GOD'S DESIGN
FOR YOUR LIFE

Thriving in Community

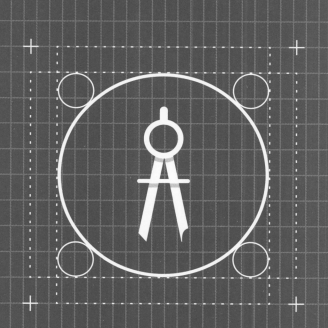

GOD'S DESIGN

FOR YOUR LIFE

Thriving in Community

GOD'S DESIGN FOR YOUR LIFE: THRIVING IN COMMUNITY

Edition 1.0

Copyright © 2014 Saddleback Church Small Groups

SADDLEBACK CHURCH

Published by Saddleback Church
1 Saddleback Parkway
Lake Forest, CA 92630
www.saddlebackresources.com

Design   Jonathan Witt
Composition Stuart Ramsey

ISBN: 978-1-4228-0272-4

Table of Contents

Help Getting Started

This video-based study is designed to be used with a group of friends at home, work, or church. It seeks to equip you and your group with basic tools to help you overcome life's challenges and thrive as a healthy and lasting community. If you're not in a small group yet, start one of your own! It's easy.

How to Start a Small Group

You don't have to be a Bible expert or teacher or even have experience in a small group. Simply keep these four steps in mind and you'll succeed as a small-group **HOST**.

- **H** ave a heart for people.
- **O** pen your home and invite a group of friends to study with you
- **S** erve them a snack
- **T** urn on the video. The video sessions will provide all of the teaching.

If you can do these four steps, you can host a small group. All of the discussion questions and next steps are provided in the study guide. Just follow along with the instructions and you'll have a great group. There's no experience necessary, so enjoy the journey.

Tips to Have a Great Small Group

Being in a small group can be scary. Most people aren't comfortable sharing what they're going through with others. We've been hurt by people close to us so we try to keep our issues to ourselves and get through. Yet one of the biggest keys to living God's design for your life is having a healthy group of friends who you are doing life with—a healthy small group. How do we create a great small group? Here are six tips.

1. Be friendly and be yourself. God wants to bless your group with the unique gifts, personality, and experiences. So be the real you with your strengths and weaknesses, don't try to be anyone else.

2. Silence is okay! When a question is asked, don't feel like you need to be the first person to jump in with an answer. Be aware of those who are quieter and give them an opportunity to share.

3. Pray for each other by name throughout the week! The inside back cover of this study guide has a "Prayers and Praises" section. Write each group member's name there so you can be praying for each other as you each face life's challenges.

4. Share responsibility for your group. One person may have signed up to host, but each person should play a role. Some may want to bring snacks or even a meal, others could help facilitate a group meeting or even host a meeting at home or lead a time of worship before the meeting. Try to find a way that you can play a role with your group.

5. Don't worry if your group doesn't have time to discuss everything in the study guide. What's most important is that you connect as a group to see what God is doing in each of your lives and how you can support each other through life's challenges.

6. Have a meeting every week, even if most of your group can't make it to the meeting. God loves to work even when only a few people come.

DESIGNED FOR RELATIONSHIPS

"

Community requires commitment. Only the Holy Spirit can create real fellowship between believers, but he cultivates it with the choices and commitments we make. Paul points out this dual responsibility when he says, *"You are joined together with peace through the Spirit, so make every effort to continue together in this way"* (Ephesians 4:3 NCV). It takes both God's power and our effort to produce a loving Christian community.

The Purpose Driven Life, Pastor Rick Warren
p. 146

Start with the first video lesson.

Designed for Relationships

> This study explores five insights we can learn from David's life on God's Design for Your Lives.

After David had finished talking with Saul, Jonathan became one in spirit with David, and he loved him as himself. . . . And Jonathan made a covenant with David because he loved him as himself. Jonathan took off the robe he was wearing and gave it to David, along with his tunic, and even his sword, his bow and his belt. 1 Samuel 18:1, 3, 4 (NIV)

> In building deep relationships we must leave our weapons, protection strategies, our masks, and quit faking "everything is okay."

We practice _____ , _____
and _____ to build
deep relationships.

The second step is letting people _____
our lives.

[David] learned that Saul had come out to take his life. And Saul's son Jonathan went to David . . . and helped him find strength in God. "Don't be afraid," he said. "My father Saul will not lay a hand on you. You will be king over Israel, and I will be second to you. Even my father Saul knows this." The two of them made a covenant before the Lord. Then Jonathan went home, but David remained at Horesh." 1 Samuel 23:15–18 (NIV)

When giving counsel to a friend we need to help them _____
_____ and
_____ for their lives.

Small Group Guidelines

Discuss these guidelines after watching the video session. It's a good idea for every group to establish and commit to a set of values and expectations in order to build a community where you can be open and honest with each other. These guidelines will help you avoid unspoken and unmet expectations and agendas. Whether you're a new group or an experienced group, reviewing these values will help your group start and stay healthy. Add anything that you feel needs to be added for your group.

Our small group's purpose is to grow healthy lives by building a healthy small group community:

A Healthy Small Group . . .

- Building relationships with others in the group
- Supporting each other's spiritual growth
- Serving each other in the group
- Inviting others to join the group
- Connecting with God through worshiping together

We agree to:

Group Attendance

- Give priority to the group meeting (call if we're absent or late).

Safe and Confidential

- Create a safe place where people can be heard and feel loved (no quick answers, snap judgments, or simple fixes). Anything that is shared is strictly confidential and within the group.

Conflict Resolution

- Avoid gossip and quickly resolve any concerns using the principles in Matthew 18:15–17.

Limit Our Freedom

- By not drinking alcohol during small group meetings or events to protect weaker brothers or sisters who have struggled with alcohol.

Sharing Roles

- Each take responsibility for part of our group, bringing snacks, hosting at our home, or facilitating group discussion.

- **Starting time** _____   **Ending Time** _____

How will we handle child care?

_____

_____

_____

_____

_____

_____

_____

Additional items

_____

_____

_____

_____

_____

_____

_____

Group Time

Icebreaker

After you've discussed the guidelines for your group, have each person share for one minute about who was his or her childhood best friend and what made them friends?

Building relationships

Now it's time to share a bit more about your life story.

Share your life story in 5 minutes with your group. Focus on your whole life picture, not just a testimony. Talk about growing up, going to school, careers, meeting a significant other, your family, your hobbies, how you got connected to your church, and when you gave your life to Jesus. If your group is larger than eight people you should break into two or more groups of four to six people to make sure everybody has time to share.

If your group has been meeting for a while, share something your group doesn't know about you. It could be an embarrassing moment, a weird job, or memorable trip, or a dream that you have for your life.

Subgrouping

Each week we're going to break into smaller, three to five person groups for some deeper sharing. Try to divide along gender lines if you're a mixed gender group. This is a great way to make sure every person has time to share and provides an opportunity for more openness.

In your subgroup share one or two areas that God is working on in your life. Have the person most comfortable with sharing go first.

Don't try to offer a quick fix or snap judgment as people share. Let people be real about what's going on in their lives. If there's something that needs prayer, don't wait until the end of the meeting, pray right then and there for them.

Prayer requests

In your subgroup share any prayer requests you have. Don't worry whether the requests are big or little. God cares about all areas of our lives. Nothing is too big for him, and nothing is too small for him. Write your requests on the inside back cover of the study guide to keep track of what God does in the lives of your group members. Then go around your circle of people and pray for the person to your right. If you've never prayed out loud in front of people just use a simple one-sentence prayer like the one below.

> "Father, Please provide a great job for Megan so her family doesn't lose their home. Amen."

Wrapping Up

Having people you can count on is the first step towards living God's design for your life. Life certainly is not always easy, but just like David had Jonathan to encourage him when life was tough, we need people who will walk with us.

One of the best practices your small group can use is subgrouping. Breaking into smaller groups helps us share deeper and builds stronger community. Remember to subgroup for prayer and discussion, especially as your group grows.

The Group Guidelines are your safety net. When someone joins, make sure to review the guidelines as a group so the new members know what the group is about.

Look at the inside front cover of the study guide for the Small Group Calendar. Divide responsibilities for the next four weeks of this study. Have group members bring snacks or a meal, host the group meeting at their home, reserve space for the group at your workplace, coffee shop or restaurant or facilitate the group time. The more people involved, the more the group becomes everyone's group, not just the host's.

Next week

Next week we'll discuss two ways David grew in his relationship with God.

DAILY
QUIET TIME

Each week of this study has five Daily Quiet Time readings to
help you grow more in your relationship with God and build a
healthy small group. Try to read and reflect on one each day.

DAY 1

One day an expert in religious law stood up to test Jesus by asking him this question: "Teacher, what should I do to inherit eternal life?" Jesus replied, "What does the law of Moses say? How do you read it?" The man answered, "You must love the Lord your God with all your heart, all your soul, all your strength, and all your mind." And, "Love your neighbor as yourself." "Right!" Jesus told him. "Do this and you will live!"

Luke 10:25–28 (NLT)

What is one way you can love your neighbor as yourself today?

DAY 2

The man wanted to justify his actions, so he asked Jesus, "And who is my neighbor?" Jesus replied with a story: "A Jewish man was traveling from Jerusalem down to Jericho, and he was attacked by bandits. They stripped him of his clothes, beat him up, and left him half dead beside the road. By chance a priest came along. But when he saw the man lying there, he crossed to the other side of the road and passed him by. A Temple assistant walked over and looked at him lying there, but he also passed by on the other side. Then a despised Samaritan came along, and when he saw the man, he felt compassion for him. Going over to him, the Samaritan soothed his wounds with olive oil and wine and bandaged them. Then he put the man on his own donkey and took him to an inn, where he took care of him. The next day he handed the innkeeper two silver coins, telling him, 'Take care of this man. If his bill runs higher than this, I'll pay you the next time I'm here.' Now which of these three would you say was a neighbor to the man who was attacked by bandits?" Jesus asked. The man replied, "The one who showed him mercy."
Then Jesus said, "Yes, now go and do the same."

Luke 10:29-37 (NLT)

Samaritans and Jews were enemies, yet the Samaritan helped
the Jewish man in need. Jesus was challenging his followers to look for
opportunities to help any one. Who can you help today?

Since you have heard about Jesus and have learned the truth that comes from him, throw off your old sinful nature and your former way of life, which is corrupted by lust and deception. Instead, let the Spirit renew your thoughts and attitudes. Put on your new nature, created to be like God—truly righteous and holy.

Ephesians 4:21–24 (NLT)

What is one area that you need the Spirit to renew your thoughts and attitudes. Ask God's Spirit to renew your thoughts and attitudes throughout your day.

*So stop telling lies. Let us tell our neighbors the truth, for we are all
parts of the same body.*

Ephesians 4:25 (NLT)

How has not telling the truth caused you to miss God's best in a
situation? How can you apply this to your small group?

DAY 5

And "don't sin by letting anger control you." Don't let the sun go down while you are still angry, for anger gives a foothold to the devil. If you are a thief, quit stealing. Instead, use your hands for good hard work, and then give generously to others in need. Don't use foul or abusive language. Let everything you say be good and helpful, so that your words will be an encouragement to those who hear them. And do not bring sorrow to God's Holy Spirit by the way you live. Remember, he has identified you as his own, guaranteeing that you will be saved on the day of redemption. Get rid of all bitterness, rage, anger, harsh words, and slander, as well as all types of evil behavior. Instead, be kind to each other, tenderhearted, forgiving one another, just as God through Christ has forgiven you.

Ephesians 4:26–32 (NLT)

What are some things you can say today that will be "good and helpful . . . an encouragement to those who hear?"

DESIGNED TO
GROW SPIRITUALLY

❝

Spiritual maturity is becoming like Jesus in the way we think, feel, and act. The more you develop Christlike character, the more you will bring glory to God. The Bible says, *"As the Spirit of the Lord works within us, we become more and more like him and reflect his glory even more."*

The Purpose Driven Life, Pastor Rick Warren
p. 59

Start with the second video lesson.

Designed to Grow Spiritually

David was, *"a man after* _____*."*

David's passion for _____ and continual
_____ marked
him as *"a man after God's Heart."*

The law of your mouth is better to me than thousands of gold and silver pieces. Your hands have made and fashioned me; give me understanding that I may learn your commandments. Those who fear you shall see me and rejoice, because I have hoped in your word. . . . Let your steadfast love comfort me according to your promise to your servant. Let your mercy come to me, that I may live; for your law is my delight. . . . I will meditate on your precepts. Let those who fear you turn to me, that they may know your testimonies. Psalm 119:72–79 (ESV)

The goal of reading the Bible is to _____
_____ in each passage.

> God's Word has promises for your life, stories of people who faced challenges and opportunities like you, instructions for building your life and revelations that show what God is really like.

I cry aloud to the Lord; I lift up my voice to the Lord for mercy. I pour out before him my complaint; before him I tell my trouble. When my spirit grows faint within me, it is you who watch over my way. In the path where I walk people have hidden a snare for me. Look and see, there is no one at my right hand; no one is concerned for me. I have no refuge; no one cares for my life. I cry to you, Lord; I say, "You are my refuge, my portion in the land of the living." Listen to my cry, for I am in desperate need; rescue me from those who pursue me, for they are too strong for me. Set me free from my prison, that I may praise your name. Psalm 142:1–7a (NIV)

Our prayers need to be _____
with God, not a religious exercise.

Then our prayers should transition to _____

_____ , _____

and _____ .

> **God is**
>
> Good
> Love
> Our Refuge
> Our Savior
> Our Healer
> Our Good Father
> Our Comforter
> Our Guide
> Our Strong Tower
> Our Protector
> Creator
> King

_____ connect, encourage
one another, and keep each other accountable to God's purpose
for their lives like Jonathan helped David.

Group Time

Icebreaker

What is your favorite Bible story? Why do you connect with that story?

_____

_____

_____

_____

_____

_____

_____

_____

_____

_____

Spiritual Health Assessment

The *Spiritual Health Assessment* is a great tool to help you measure how you are doing with five different areas of our spiritual lives: relationships, spiritual growth habits, serving, worship, and evangelism. You can download the app from **www. SpiritualHealthApp.com** or the Apple and Android app stores by searching "Transform Me" to complete the assessment on your phone or tablet. You can find the paper version on page 80 in the Appendix. Simply answer the questions and then add up the scores for each area of spiritual health and identify where you are strong and weak. Don't compare your score to others! Some people give themselves higher scores while others reserve the highest scores only for Jesus. The assessment helps you identify your relative strengths and weaknesses.

If your group has been together for a while you may want to have one of your group members do the assessment for you as well. Having feedback from others can help us identify the blind spots in our lives.

Finally choose a next step in one or two of the areas. The first two weeks of this study are about relationships and growing spiritually so you may want to pick a next step in those areas.

Come back together as a group once you've completed your Health Assessment and picked one or two next steps.

Subgrouping

Break into smaller groups if your group is larger than eight. Breaking up along gender lines is always best if your group is a mixed gender group. Then discuss the following questions:

Which area did you score highest in the assessment?

_____

_____

_____

_____

In what way could you help serve in your group in that area? Be creative or pick one way to serve your group from the list below over the next few weeks and write it on the Small Group Calendar on the inside front cover of the study guide.

_____

_____

_____

_____

_____

_____

_____

Ideas for serving

Fellowship

- Host or organize a group get together on a weekend.

Discipleship

- Facilitate one of the group meetings for this study.

Ministry

- Help organize the group to serve a group member or someone else in need.

Evangelism

- Help organize a party for the end of this study to invite people who don't know Jesus to join your group

Worship

- Select a worship song to begin each group meeting. Play it on an instrument or watch it on YouTube®.

Which area of the Health Assessment did you score lowest? What is your next step in that area?

_____

_____

_____

_____

_____

_____

_____

_____

_____

_____

_____

_____

Spiritual partners

Now divide your group into smaller groups of two or three. The other person or people in your group of two or three will be your Spiritual Partners for this study. Write their names below along with the next step each person has shared. You'll be checking in next week to encourage each other and see how you're doing with the next step.

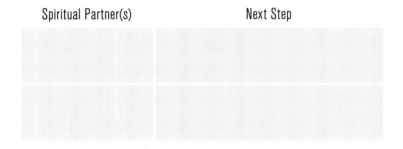

Spiritual Partner(s)	Next Step

With your spiritual partners, share any prayer requests and write them down on the inside of the front cover of this study guide.

Take time to pray for each other. If you're nervous about praying out loud, use a simple one line prayer like,

> "Father, please give Joe wisdom about whether or not to take the new job he was offered."

Wrapping Up

If you truly want to grow spiritually in this small group, simply watching a DVD and talking about what you think about it won't grow you enough. Growth happens as the Holy Spirit works in and with you as you make a commitment in an area and stick to it. Spiritual partners are the most effective way to ensure you stick to your commitments. Even after this study ends, it is a good idea to plan time during the group meetings to connect with your spiritual partners to encourage each other.

The Spiritual Health Assessment or Transform Me app is a powerful tool to help you spot areas of strength from which you can serve others and areas of weakness that you can work on. Healthy small groups take the assessment every four to six months to review how they're doing and establish new goals.

Next week

Next week we'll see how God used David's personality and experiences to prepare him to defeat his giants.

Daily
Quiet Time

Growing in your relationship with God is dependent upon spending daily time with him in his Word, reflecting on what he shows you there, and talking to him in prayer about how you should respond. Each week of this study has five Daily Quiet Time readings to help you grow more in your relationship with God and to build a healthy small group. Try to read and reflect on one each day.

DAY 1

Two are better than one, because they have a good return for their labor: If either of them falls down, one can help the other up. But pity anyone who falls and has no one to help them up. Also, if two lie down together, they will keep warm. But how can one keep warm alone? Though one may be overpowered, two can defend themselves. A cord of three strands is not quickly broken.

Ecclesiastes 4:9–12 (NIV)

Who are the people in your life who come to mind when you read this? How can you strengthen your spiritual partners this week?

DAY 2

Oh, how I love your law! I meditate on it all day long. Your commands are always with me and make me wiser than my enemies. I have more insight than all my teachers, for I meditate on your statutes. I have more understanding than the elders, for I obey your precepts. I have kept my feet from every evil path so that I might obey your word. I have not departed from your laws, for you yourself have taught me. How sweet are your words to my taste, sweeter than honey to my mouth! I gain understanding from your precepts; therefore I hate every wrong path. Your word is a lamp for my feet, a light on my path.

Psalm 119:97–105 (NIV)

Write down a verse or phrase from the first two weeks' Daily Quiet Time sections on a note card or sticky note. Put it somewhere that you will see it multiple times in your day and meditate on what it means.

DAY 3

My heart is in anguish within me; the terrors of death have fallen upon me. Fear and trembling come upon me, and horror overwhelms me. But I call to God, and the Lord will save me. Evening and morning and at noon I utter my complaint and moan, and he hears my voice.

Psalm 55:4, 5, 16, 17 (ESV)

It's never bad to complain to God; he wants you to be honest in your prayer. Spend time telling God what you really think about the giants in your life. Then shift your focus to how he hears and saves you.

DAY 4

Let us hold tightly without wavering to the hope we affirm, for God can be trusted to keep his promise. Let us think of ways to motivate one another to acts of love and good works. And let us not neglect our meeting together, as some people do, but encourage one another, especially now that the day of his return is drawing near.

Hebrews 10:23–25 (NLT)

How can we motivate one another to acts of love and good works within our small group?

DAY 5

[Then Jesus said] *"Pray along these lines: 'Our Father in heaven, we honor your holy name. We ask that your kingdom will come now. May your will be done here on earth, just as it is in heaven. Give us our food again today, as usual, and forgive us our sins, just as we have forgiven those who have sinned against us. Don't bring us into temptation, but deliver us from the Evil One.'"*

Matthew 6:9–13 (TLB)

Jesus modeled another way to pray. Pray the prayer but add to each segment your own prayers. For example, after "Our Father in heaven, we honor your holy name," spend a minute thinking and praying about other attributes of God. After "Give us our food again," make specific requests for needs you have.

DESIGNED TO
SERVE OTHERS

“

Like stained glass, our different personalities reflect God's light in many colors and patterns. This blesses the family of God with depth and variety. It also blesses us personally. It feels good to do what God made you to do.

The Purpose Driven Life, Pastor Rick Warren
p. 243–244

Start with the third video lesson.

Designed to Serve Others

Now the Israelites had been saying, "Do you see how this man keeps coming out? He comes out to defy Israel. The king will give great wealth to the man who kills him. He will also give him his daughter in marriage and will exempt his family from taxes in Israel."

David asked the men standing near him, "What will be done for the man who kills this Philistine and removes this disgrace from Israel? Who is this uncircumcised Philistine that he should defy the armies of the living God?"

They repeated to him what they had been saying and told him, "This is what will be done for the man who kills him."

When Eliab, David's oldest brother, heard him speaking with the men, he burned with anger at him and asked, "Why have you come down here? And with whom did you leave those few sheep in the wilderness? I know how conceited you are and how wicked your heart is; you came down only to watch the battle." 1 Samuel 17:25–27 (NIV)

God has given each of us a _____
according to his design for our life.

> It's important to realize that our personality is God-given and that he wants us to live the way he created us.

"Let no one lose heart on account of this Philistine; your servant will go and fight him." Saul replied, "You are not able to go out against this Philistine and fight him; you are only a young man, and he has been a warrior from his youth."

But David said to Saul, "Your servant has been keeping his father's sheep. When a lion or a bear came and carried off a sheep from the flock, I went after it, struck it and rescued the sheep from its mouth.

When it turned on me, I seized it by its hair, struck it and killed it. Your servant has killed both the lion and the bear; this uncircumcised Philistine will be like one of them, because he has defied the armies of the living God. The Lord who rescued me from the paw of the lion and the paw of the bear will rescue me from the hand of this Philistine. 1 Samuel 17:32–37 (NIV)

Our _____ prepare us for the impossibilities that we will face.

Your _____ equips you to _____ to others going through similar experiences.

Saul said to David, "Go, and the Lord be with you."

Then he took his staff in his hand, chose five smooth stones from the stream, put them in the pouch of his shepherd's bag and, with his sling in his hand, approached the Philistine. Meanwhile, the Philistine, with his shield bearer in front of him, kept coming closer to David. He looked David over and saw that he was little more than a boy, glowing with health and handsome, and he despised him. He said to David, "Am I a dog, that you come at me with sticks?"

And the Philistine cursed David by his gods. "Come here," he said, "and I'll give your flesh to the birds and the wild animals!"

David said to the Philistine, "You come against me with sword and spear and javelin, but I come against you in the name of the Lord Almighty, the God of the armies of Israel, whom you have defied. This day the Lord will deliver you into my hands, and I'll strike you down and cut off your head. This very day I will give the carcasses of the Philistine army to the birds and the wild animals, and the whole world will know that there is a God in Israel. All those gathered here will know that it is not by sword or spear that the Lord saves; for the battle is the Lord's, and he will give all of you into our hands."

As the Philistine moved closer to attack him, David ran quickly toward the battle line to meet him. Reaching into his bag and taking out a stone, he slung it and struck the Philistine on the forehead. The stone sank into his forehead, and he fell facedown on the ground. So David triumphed over the Philistine with a sling and a stone; without a sword in his hand he struck down the Philistine and killed him.
1 Samuel 17: 37c, 40–50 (NIV)

Relying on _____ is the best way to get killed when facing our giants. We must depend on _____ .

Group Time

Icebreaker

Four different personality scales are listed below. Spend a minute sharing where you fit on each of the scales.

1................2................3................4................5
Introverted   Extroverted
Energized from alone time   Energized from being with people

1................2................3................4................5
Organized   Spontaneous
Prefer life to be orderly and routine   Prefer life to be varied and messy

1................2................3................4................5
Thinker   Feeler
Base decision on "facts" not "feelings"   Base decisions on others feelings

1................2................3................4................5
Big Picture   Details
Like dreaming about what could be   Enjoy figuring out specifics of the now

What do you like about your personality?

What would you like to change about your personality?

Is what you'd like to change something you think God would like you to change?

Sometimes we take a strength too far, like an organized person becoming a perfectionist. Other times we let fear get in the way of our personality. God gave us our personality, but we do need to ensure that we don't let our strengths become weaknesses or let fear cripple us.

Subgrouping

Just like God used David's experience fighting lions and bears, he can use our scary and painful experiences to help us serve others.

Break into subgroups of three to five people. In your subgroups, share for a few minutes about one of your personal painful experiences that God could use to help others.

Spiritual partner check in

Now partner up with your spiritual partner(s). Look back on your next step from the last lesson. Talk about how you did this past week. Is there any way you can help each other do better this week?

> Often times texting (SMS messaging) is a great way to assist each other either by checking in or asking for prayer when a challenge or temptation arises.

Choose a next step from this week's discussion. How are you going to use your personality or experiences to help serve others around you?

Share prayer requests and updates from a previous week's requests. Celebrate the answered prayers together. Then spend time praying for each other.

Wrapping Up

God has given us a personality and experiences that equip us to serve others inside and outside of our small group. Always be on the lookout for ways to serve each other in the group. Look for ways your group can serve together either in your community or at your church.

Next week

Next week we will examine David's highest priority, connecting with God through worship. We will take communion together so have someone in your group bring grape juice and crackers or bread to the group meeting.

Daily
Quiet Time

Each week of this study has five Daily Quiet Time readings to help
you grow more in your relationship with God and build a healthy
small group. Try to read and reflect on one each day.

DAY 1

Then Saul dressed David in his own tunic. He put a coat of armor on him and a bronze helmet on his head. David fastened on his sword over the tunic and tried walking around, because he was not used to them. "I cannot go in these," he said to Saul, "because I am not used to them." So he took them off. Then he took his staff in his hand, chose five smooth stones from the stream, put them in the pouch of his shepherd's bag and, with his sling in his hand, approached the Philistine

1 Samuel 17:38-40 (NIV)

Saul tried to have David wear his armor to fight Goliath, but David refused. He was successful in his fight using the tools he was used to. How have you aligned your life to meet the expectations of others instead of being who God created you to be?

DAY 2

Just as our bodies have many parts and each part has a special function, so it is with Christ's body. We are many parts of one body, and we all belong to each other. In his grace, God has given us different gifts for doing certain things well. So if God has given you the ability to prophesy, speak out with as much faith as God has given you. If your gift is serving others, serve them well. If you are a teacher, teach well. If your gift is to encourage others, be encouraging. If it is giving, give generously. If God has given you leadership ability, take the responsibility seriously. And if you have a gift for showing kindness to others, do it gladly.

Romans 12:4–8 NLT

What gifts and abilities has God given you to help others in your small group and church?

DAY 3

Don't just pretend to love others. Really love them. Hate what is wrong. Hold tightly to what is good. Love each other with genuine affection, and take delight in honoring each other. Never be lazy, but work hard and serve the Lord enthusiastically. Rejoice in our confident hope. Be patient in trouble, and keep on praying. When God's people are in need, be ready to help them. Always be eager to practice hospitality.

Romans 12:9–13 NLT

Who is in need in your small group or circle of friends? How can you "really love them" and help them?

Bless those who persecute you. Don't curse them; pray that God will bless them. Be happy with those who are happy, and weep with those who weep. Live in harmony with each other. Don't be too proud to enjoy the company of ordinary people. And don't think you know it all! Never pay back evil with more evil. Do things in such a way that everyone can see you are honorable. Do all that you can to live in peace with everyone. Dear friends, never take revenge. Leave that to the righteous anger of God. For the Scriptures say, "I will take revenge; I will pay them back," says the Lord. Instead, "If your enemies are hungry, feed them. If they are thirsty, give them something to drink. In doing this, you will heap burning coals of shame on their heads." Don't let evil conquer you, but conquer evil by doing good.

Romans 12:14–21 NLT

Our pain can make us bitter or better. What painful experience do you need to redeem by doing good?

DAY 5

The Lord gave me this message: "I knew you before I formed you in your mother's womb. Before you were born I set you apart and appointed you as my prophet to the nations." "O Sovereign Lord," I said, "I can't speak for you! I'm too young!" The Lord replied, "Don't say, 'I'm too young,' for you must go wherever I send you and say whatever I tell you. And don't be afraid of the people, for I will be with you and will protect you. I, the Lord, have spoken!"

Jeremiah 1:4-8 NLT

God called Jeremiah as a prophet, yet Jeremiah was scared.
In which situation do you need to not be afraid and know that God is
with you and will protect you?

DESIGNED TO
CONNECT WITH GOD

“

Knowing and loving God is our greatest privilege, and being known and loved is God's greatest pleasure. God says, if any want to boast that they know and understand me. . . . These are the things that please me.

The Purpose Driven Life, Pastor Rick Warren

p. 89

Watch the video lesson and story now.

Designed to Connect with God

> David's connection with God enabled him to live out God's design for his life.

One thing I ask from the Lord, this only do I seek: that I may dwell in the house of the Lord all the days of my life, to gaze on the beauty of the Lord and to seek him in his temple. Psalm 27:4 (NIV)

When we _____ we connect with God.

The heavens declare the glory of God; the skies proclaim the work of his hands. Psalm 19:1 (NIV)

The Lord is gracious and compassionate, slow to anger and rich in love. The Lord is good to all; he has compassion on all he has made. The Lord is trustworthy in all he promises and faithful in all he does. The Lord upholds all who fall and lifts up all who are bowed down. The eyes of all look to you, and you give them their food at the proper time. You open your hand and satisfy the desires of every living thing. The Lord is righteous in all his ways and faithful in all he does. The Lord is near to all who call on him, to all who call on him in truth. He fulfills the desires of those who fear him; he hears their cry and saves them. The Lord watches over all who love him, but all the wicked he will destroy. Psalm 145:8, 9, 13b–20 (NIV)

As you read God's Word, look for scriptures that _____

_____ .

Anyone who belongs to Christ has become a new person. 2 Corinthians 5:17 (NLT)

Remembering _____ in   our
lives helps us connect with God. _____ is an
act of remembering what Jesus did for us on the cross.

"Jesus, on the night he was betrayed, took bread, and when he had
given thanks, he broke it and said, "This is my body, which is for you;
do this in remembrance of me." In the same way, after supper he took
the cup, saying, "This cup is the new covenant in my blood; do this,
whenever you drink it, in remembrance of me." 1 Corinthians
11:23b–25 (NIV)

If we are to take the Lord's Supper, we must be _____

_____ .

We must _____ before we
take communion.

Group Time

Icebreaker

In one minute, describe your favorite way and place to connect with God.

Worship time

Start by spending time individually, quietly re-reading the verses from Psalm 145 found on page 48. Pause after each line and reflect on what it reveals about God. After five minutes come together as a group; each of you share one thing that spoke to you from your time of reflection in Psalm 145.

> Reading and reflecting on scripture or songs together is a great way to incorporate worship into your group meetings and help your group connect with God together.

Now listen to the song "Our Hope" on the DVD or video streaming page. Again reflect on what it reveals about God. Meditate on the message in the song for a minute after it finishes playing. Then briefly share which of God's traits you need to hold onto in your current season of life.

Communion

Pour a small amount of grape juice into enough cups for each person in your group to have one. Then break up crackers or bread so each person can have a small piece. Play the communion video provided with this session and take communion together as the pastor leads it.

> Taking communion together as a group is a great way to remember what God has done in your group. You should celebrate communion as a group every six to eight weeks helps keep Jesus at the center of your group.

Subgrouping

Spiritual partner check in

Break into your spiritual partner groups of two or three. Look back at your next step from last week. Talk about how you did since our last meeting. Is there any way you can help each other do better this week?

Choose a next step from this week's discussion. How will you spend time connecting with God?

Share prayer requests and updates from last week's requests. Celebrate the answered prayers together. Then spend time praying for each other.

Wrapping Up

We all need to live in connection with God so we can live out God's design for our life. Worship can be a part of every small group meeting. We can listen to or sing a song together, meditate on scripture, take communion, or spend an extended time praying together to intentionally connect with God. All of these activities invite him into the challenges we are facing and enable us to see that he is bigger than the giants we are facing.

Next week

Next week we're going to discuss how David shared stories of what God had done in his life.

Daily
Quiet Time

Each week of this study has five Daily Quiet Time readings to help
you grow more in your relationship with God and build a healthy
small group. Try to read and reflect on one each day.

Love is patient, love is kind. It does not envy, it does not boast, it is not proud. It does not dishonor others, it is not self-seeking, it is not easily angered, it keeps no record of wrongs. Love does not delight in evil but rejoices with the truth. It always protects, always trusts, always hopes, always perseveres. Love never fails.

1 Corinthians 13:4–8a (NIV)

1 John 4:8 says that God is love. Reread these verses substituting God for Love and "it" where it applies to love. How is this picture of God different from the picture you've had of him?

DAY 2

The Lord is my shepherd. I am never in need. He makes me lie down in green pastures. He leads me beside peaceful waters. He renews my soul. He guides me along the paths of righteousness for the sake of his name. Even though I walk through the dark valley of death, because you are with me, I fear no harm. Your rod and your staff give me courage. You prepare a banquet for me while my enemies watch. You anoint my head with oil. My cup overflows. Certainly, goodness and mercy will stay close to me all the days of my life, and I will remain in the Lord's house for days without end.

Psalm 23 (GWT)

Spend time reflecting on this verse, "Even though I walk through the dark valley of death, because you are with me, I fear no harm." How can you apply this to dark valleys you are facing?

DAY 3

Jesus continued: "There was a man who had two sons. The younger one said to his father, 'Father, give me my share of the estate.' So he divided his property between them. "Not long after that, the younger son got together all he had, set off for a distant country and there squandered his wealth in wild living. After he had spent everything, there was a severe famine in that whole country, and he began to be in need. So he went and hired himself out to a citizen of that country, who sent him to his fields to feed pigs. He longed to fill his stomach with the pods that the pigs were eating, but no one gave him anything. "When he came to his senses, he said, 'How many of my father's hired servants have food to spare, and here I am starving to death! I will set out and go back to my father and say to him: Father, I have sinned against heaven and against you. I am no longer worthy to be called your son; make me like one of your hired servants.' So he got up and went to his father. "But while he was still a long way off, his father saw him and was filled with compassion for him; he ran to his son, threw his arms around him and kissed him. "The son said to him, 'Father, I have sinned against heaven and against you. I am no longer worthy to be called your son.' "But the father said to his servants, 'Quick! Bring the best robe and put it on him. Put a ring on his finger and sandals on his feet. Bring the fattened calf and kill it. Let's have a feast and celebrate. For this son of mine was dead and is alive again; he was lost and is found.' So they began to celebrate.

Luke 15:11–24 (NIV)

Jesus used this story to show what Father God is like, how he is waiting for us to come back to him. How has he welcomed you back even when you haven't followed him well?

DAY 4

Do not be afraid, because I have reclaimed you. I have called you by name; you are mine. When you go through the sea, I am with you. When you go through rivers, they will not sweep you away. When you walk through fire, you will not be burned, and the flames will not harm you. I am the Lord your God, the Holy One of Israel, your Savior. Since you are precious to me, you are honored and I love you.

Isaiah 43:1b–3a, 4a (GWT)

God doesn't promise we won't go through trials. This passage says "when" we go through trials God is with us. Meditate on the promises in these verses. How can you remember his promises in the midst of facing life's giants?

DAY 5

After [Paul and Silas] *had been severely flogged, they were thrown into prison, and the jailer was commanded to guard them carefully. About midnight Paul and Silas were praying and singing hymns to God, and the other prisoners were listening to them. Suddenly there was such a violent earthquake that the foundations of the prison were shaken. At once all the prison doors flew open, and everyone's chains came loose. The jailer woke up, and when he saw the prison doors open, he drew his sword and was about to kill himself because he thought the prisoners had escaped. But Paul shouted, "Don't harm yourself! We are all here!" The jailer called for lights, rushed in and fell trembling before Paul and Silas. He then brought them out and asked, "Sirs, what must I do to be saved?" They replied, "Believe in the Lord Jesus, and you will be saved—you and your household." Then they spoke the word of the Lord to him and to all the others in his house. At that hour of the night the jailer took them and washed their wounds; then immediately he and all his household were baptized. The jailer brought them into his house and set a meal before them; he was filled with joy because he had come to believe in God—he and his whole household.*

Acts 16:23, 24–34 (NIV)

God used worship to bring freedom to Paul and Silas and salvation to the jailer and his family. For which situation in your life do you need to worship more and let God do what only he can do?

DESIGNED TO
SHARE YOUR STORY

66

Jesus said, "You will be my witnesses" . . . He wants you to share your story with others . . . There is no other story just like yours, so only you can share it. If you don't share it, it will be lost forever."

The Purpose Driven Life, **Pastor Rick Warren**
p. 288

Watch the fifth video lesson

Designed to Share Your Story

"[The Lord] *reached down from on high and took hold of me; he drew me out of deep waters. He rescued me from my powerful enemy, from my foes, who were too strong for me. They confronted me in the day of my disaster, but the Lord was my support. He brought me out into a spacious place; he rescued me because he delighted in me.* 2 Samuel 22:17–20 NIV

One generation commends your works to another; they tell of your mighty acts. They speak of the glorious splendor of your majesty— They tell of the power of your awesome works—and I will proclaim your great deeds. They tell of the glory of your kingdom and speak of your might, so that all people may know of your mighty acts and the glorious splendor of your kingdom. Psalm 145:4–5a, 6, 11–12 NIV

> Sharing the stories of what God has done helps strengthen our relationship with him, encourages others who know him and help people who don't know Jesus come to know him.

We need to share the _____

_____ in our lives.

Sharing your story

> Start with life before you knew Jesus.
>
> Then share how and why you asked Jesus to be your savior.
>
> End with telling the difference Jesus has made in your life, what means the most to you personally.

There should always be room for _____

_____ .

I can invite _____

to the group.

When someone joins your small group, _____

_____ of what God has done in your lives.

The future of this group

You've seen and experienced a taste of what God can do in your life through being in a small group. Having a group of people with whom you are doing life together is one of the most powerful keys to overcome life's challenges. With this study almost over, spend some time discussing the future of your group. Experiencing the power of community like David and the people who shared their stories on the video takes time and commitment. The same will be true for your small group.

> Elect a Group Contact Person who will be in charge of connecting with your church to get support, resources, and prayer for your group. Specify that person on the Small Group Commitment with their contact information.

Before your group continues with this study, have one group member go to GodsDesign.co on their mobile device. Select the "Small Group Commitment" banner. Review and complete the commitment as a group. Then continue with the rest of this session.

Group Time

Icebreaker

When did you come to know Jesus? If you are not sure that you really know Jesus yet, take a minute or so to share your hopes for your time in this group/study.

Share the five minute version of your story of what God has done in your life. Use the outline provided in the video session if you're unsure about what to say. You may want to take notes on other group members' stories as they share what God has done in their lives.

Small Group Party!

Next week, during your group time or during the weekend, host a small group party! Whether you go out to eat or have a potluck dinner or hors d'oeuvre, enjoy food and invite others who could join your group. It's always good to focus on people who aren't religious and don't attend church. You might want to spend time sharing stories of what God has done in your lives through the study and your group; or you can wait until the next time they visit your group. Either way, make a connection with each other's friends and see what God does.

To help you identify people you can invite to the party spend five minutes identifying activities that you're currently involved in. Then write down a few names of people you connect with during those activities

Activities You Enjoy	People to Invite
(hobbies, sports, work, kids, clubs, etc.)	(friends, family, coworkers, etc.)
_____	_____
_____	_____
_____	_____
_____	_____

Now select one or two people on your list and invite them to your party next week. Share who you will invite with your group.

Spiritual Partner Check In

Break into your spiritual partner groups of two or three.

Look back on your next step from last week. Talk about how you did this past week. Is there a way you can help each other do better this week?

_____

_____

_____

_____

_____

Choose a next step from this week's discussion. Who are you going to invite to your group party next week?

_____

_____

_____

_____

_____

Share prayer requests and updates from previous prayer requests. Celebrate the answered prayers together. Then spend time praying for each other.

Wrapping Up

Be sure to discuss and fill out the Small Group Commitment form. Your church wants to know your group is continuing and will help provide support, resources and prayer.

Inviting someone to one of your small group events could be critical in helping them come to know Jesus. Always be thinking of who you can invite to join you for your next group event.

When a new person joins your group, devote a meeting to sharing your stories. It helps build connections and can help them discover God's love, maybe for the first time.

Next Week

Next week plan to invite other people to your group party who could benefit from being a part of your group. Remember to think about people who aren't religious and don't attend church. Even if they are unable to come to your group party, share the story of the difference Jesus has made in your life with those people.

Daily
Quiet Time

Each week of this study has five Daily Quiet Time readings to help you grow more in your relationship with God and build a healthy small group. Try to read and reflect on one each day.

DAY 1

We proclaim to you the one who existed from the beginning, whom we have heard and seen. We saw him with our own eyes and touched him with our own hands. He is the Word of life. This one who is life itself was revealed to us, and we have seen him. And now we testify and proclaim to you that he is the one who is eternal life. He was with the Father, and then he was revealed to us. We proclaim to you what we ourselves have actually seen and heard so that you may have fellowship with us. And our fellowship is with the Father and with his Son, Jesus Christ. We are writing these things so that you may fully share our joy.

1 John 1:1-4 (NLT)

The man who wrote this, John, got to actually touch
and see Jesus as he followed him. We too can share what we
have seen, heard and experienced in our own lives. Who can you share
your story with so they may share your joy?

DAY 2

This is the message we heard from Jesus and now declare to you: God is light, and there is no darkness in him at all. So we are lying if we say we have fellowship with God but go on living in spiritual darkness; we are not practicing the truth. But if we are living in the light, as God is in the light, then we have fellowship with each other, and the blood of Jesus, his Son, cleanses us from all sin. If we claim we have no sin, we are only fooling ourselves and not living in the truth. But if we confess our sins to him, he is faithful and just to forgive us our sins and to cleanse us from all wickedness. If we claim we have not sinned, we are calling God a liar and showing that his word has no place in our hearts

1 John 1:5-10 (NLT)

When sharing your story, this passage shows how we can come to know Jesus. "If we confess our sins to him, he is faithful and just to forgive us our sins and to cleanse us from all wickedness." Spend time memorizing that verse, 1 John 1:9.

DAY 3

And [Jesus] *said, "Yes, it was written long ago that the Messiah would suffer and die and rise from the dead on the third day. It was also written that this message would be proclaimed in the authority of his name to all the nations, beginning in Jerusalem: 'There is forgiveness of sins for all who repent.' You are witnesses of all these things. "And now I will send the Holy Spirit, just as my Father promised. But stay here in the city until the Holy Spirit comes and fills you with power from heaven." Then Jesus led them to Bethany, and lifting his hands to heaven, he blessed them. While he was blessing them, he left them and was taken up to heaven. So they worshiped him and then returned to Jerusalem filled with great joy.*

Luke 24:46-52 (NLT)

For us to be effective witnesses, Jesus said we need the Holy Spirit to empower us. Ask the Holy Spirit to fill you and give you the wisdom, guidance and power to effectively share your story.

As [Peter and John] *approached the Temple, a man lame from birth was being carried in. Each day he was put beside the Temple gate, the one called the Beautiful Gate, so he could beg from the people going into the Temple. The lame man looked at them eagerly, expecting some money. But Peter said, "I don't have any silver or gold for you. But I'll give you what I have. In the name of Jesus Christ the Nazarene, get up and walk!" Then Peter took the lame man by the right hand and helped him up. And as he did, the man's feet and ankles were instantly healed and strengthened. He jumped up, stood on his feet, and began to walk! Then, walking, leaping, and praising God, he went into the Temple with them. All the people saw him walking and heard him praising God. When they realized he was the lame beggar they had seen so often at the Beautiful Gate, they were absolutely astounded! They all rushed out in amazement to Solomon's Colonnade, where the man was holding tightly to Peter and John.*

Acts 3:2, 5–11 NLT

Many people came to know and believe in Jesus as Savior because they saw the difference Jesus made in the lame man's life. Who knew you before you knew Jesus and would be amazed at what he's done in your life? Reconnect with them and share the story of what Jesus has done.

DAY 5

While Peter and John were speaking to the people, they were confronted by the priests, the captain of the Temple guard, and some of the Sadducees. These leaders were very disturbed that Peter and John were teaching the people that through Jesus there is a resurrection of the dead. They arrested them and, since it was already evening, put them in jail until morning. The members of the council were amazed when they saw the boldness of Peter and John, for they could see that they were ordinary men with no special training in the Scriptures. They also recognized them as men who had been with Jesus. But since they could see the man who had been healed standing right there among them, there was nothing the council could say.

Acts 4:1–3, 13, 14 NLT

God's chosen people are often ordinary with no special training,
yet they can be recognized as people who have been changed by Jesus.
What will it take for others to see Jesus through your life?

Helpful
Materials

Answer Key

Session 1

We practice openness, honesty and vulnerability to build deep relationships.

The second step is letting people speak into our lives.

When giving counsel to a friend we need to help them connect with God and remember his purpose for their lives.

Session 2

David was "a man after God's heart."

David's passion for God's Word and continual conversation with God marked him as "a man after God's heart."

The goal of reading the Bible is to discover the treasure in each passage.

Our prayers need to be open and honest with God, not a religious exercise.

Then our prayers should transition to remembering who God is, what he is like and what his promises are.

Spiritual partners connect, encourage each other and keep each other accountable to God's purpose for their lives.

Session 3

God has given each of us a unique personality to equip us for the challenges we face.

Our experiences prepare us for the impossibilities that we will face.

Your pain equips you to minister to others going through similar experiences.

Relying on ourselves is the best way to get killed when facing our giants. We must depend on God.

Session 4

When we meditate on what God's like we connect with God.

As you read God's word, look for scriptures that reveal what God is like.

Remembering what God has done in our lives helps us connect with God.

Communion is an act of remembering what Jesus did for us on the cross.

If we are to take the Lord's Supper, we must be followers of Jesus.

We must examine ourselves before we take communion.

Session 5

We need to share the stories of what God has done in our lives.

There should always be room for one more person in our group.

When someone joins your small group, share the stories of what God has done in your lives.

FAQ

How long will this group meet?

This study is five sessions long. We encourage your group to add a sixth session to invite others who might be interested in joining your group. When you've finished with this study there are more in-depth studies in the *Healthy Small Group Series* to help your group grow to become a healthy and lasting small group. They're available through your small group community leader, coach or small group pastor, or through **www.SaddlebackResources.com.**

How do we handle childcare in our group?

Childcare needs must be handled very carefully as it's a sensitive issue. Having kids running around and crying during the meeting is very distracting. If kids are old enough to sit and participate, some groups choose to have their children as a part of the group. Others have the group meeting in the living room and a baby sitter (or two) in another room watching the children, they split the cost of the baby sitter. Another option is to have one home for the adults and another nearby home for the kids. If a babysitter doesn't work, adults can take turns watching the children together. We recommend having two ladies or two men watch the kids together so they can connect while watching the children. If the kids are older, they may want to provide a lesson for the kids.

Finding New Group Members

Use the circles below to help identify people you can invite to your small group.

1. Simply list one or two people in each circle

2. Prayerfully select one or two of the people from your list and tell your group about them.

3. Invite that person to your group meeting or group party. Over fifty percent of people invited to a small group say, "Yes."

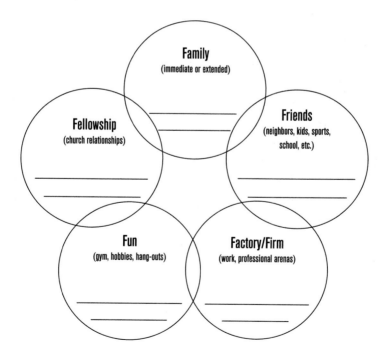

Spiritual Health Assessment

The Spiritual Health Assessment is designed to help you evaluate how you are doing in each of God's five purposes for your life, the five areas that this study focuses on, and create a plan to improve your weaknesses and serve in your strengths. The assessment is also available as the *Transform Me* app at **www. SpiritualHealthApp.com** if you prefer to do it on your mobile device.

Instructions

1. Rate yourself on each of the statements from 0 to 5, with zero meaning the statement doesn't match you and five meaning it is a strong match.

2. After you have rated each statement, add the results by transferring your ratings from each of the statements to the scoring table on this page. Then add up the numbers in each column to find your score for each purpose.

3. Then use the Spiritual Health Plan on page 83 to create a plan to help you grow spiritually.

Test yourselves to make sure you are solid in the faith. Don't drift along taking everything for granted. Give yourselves regular checkups . . . Test it out. If you fail the test, do something about it. 2 Corinthians 13:5 (MSG)

The Spiritual Health Assessment and Spiritual Health Planner measures your health at a particular point in time. It is not a tool to see how you measure up against other people; nor is it a tool to see how close you are to perfection. We all know we'll never be perfect this side of heaven. Rather, this is a tool that will help you evaluate your spiritual health, and give you direction for developing a plan to bring God's five purposes for your life into balance.

	Doesn't Match	Partial Match	Strong Match

Worship: Designed to Connect with God

How I live my life shows that God is my highest priority 0 1 2 3 4 5

I am dependent on God for every aspect of my life 0 1 2 3 4 5

There is nothing in my life that I have not surrendered to (kept back from) God ... 0 1 2 3 4 5

I regularly meditate on God's Word and invite Him into my everyday activities 0 1 2 3 4 5

I have a deep desire to spend time in God's presence 0 1 2 3 4 5

I am the same person in public that I am in private 0 1 2 3 4 5

I have an overwhelming sense of God's awesomeness even when

I do not feel His presence 0 1 2 3 4 5

Worship Total _____

Fellowship: Designed for Relationships

I am genuinely open and honest about who I am 0 1 2 3 4 5

I regularly use my time and resources to care for the needs of others 0 1 2 3 4 5

I have a deep and meaningful connection with others in the church........... 0 1 2 3 4 5

I have an easy time receiving advice, encouragement, and correction from others 0 1 2 3 4 5

I gather regularly with a group of Christians for fellowship and accountability.... 0 1 2 3 4 5

There is nothing in my relationships that is currently unresolved 0 1 2 3 4 5

There is nothing in the way I talk or act concerning others that I would

not be willing to share with them in person 0 1 2 3 4 5

Fellowship Total _____

Discipleship: Designed to Grow Spiritually

I am quick to confess anything in my character that does not look like Christ.... 0 1 2 3 4 5

A review of how I use my finances shows that I think more about God

and others than I do about myself................................. 0 1 2 3 4 5

I allow God's Word to guide my thoughts and change my actions 0 1 2 3 4 5

I am able to praise God during difficult times and see them as opportunities to grow .. 0 1 2 3 4 5

I find I am making better choices to do what is right when I am tempted to do wrong . 0 1 2 3 4 5

I have found that prayer has changed how I view and interact with the world 0 1 2 3 4 5

I am consistent in pursuing habits that are helping me model my life after Jesus 0 1 2 3 4 5

Discipleship Total _____

	Doesn't Match	Partial Match	Strong Match

Ministry: Designed to Serve Others

I regularly use my time to serve God. 0 1 2 3 4 5

I am currently serving God with the gifts and passions he has given me 0 1 2 3 4 5

I regularly reflect on how my life can have an impact for the Kingdom of God . . . 0 1 2 3 4 5

I enjoy meeting the needs of others without expecting anything in return 0 1 2 3 4 5

I often think about ways to use my God-given gifts and abilities to please God . . . 0 1 2 3 4 5

Those closest to me would say my life is a reflection of giving more than receiving 0 1 2 3 4 5

I see my painful experiences as opportunities to minister to others 0 1 2 3 4 5

Ministry Total   _____

Evangelism: Designed to Share the Story

I feel personal responsibility to share my faith with those who don't know Jesus . 0 1 2 3 4 5

I look for opportunities to build relationships with those who don't know Jesus . . 0 1 2 3 4 5

I regularly pray for those who don't know Christ 0 1 2 3 4 5

I am confident in my ability to share my faith 0 1 2 3 4 5

My heart is full of passion to share the good news of the gospel with
    those who have never heard it 0 1 2 3 4 5

I find that my relationship with Jesus comes up frequently in my
    conversations with those who don't know him 0 1 2 3 4 5

I am open to going anywhere God calls me, in whatever capacity,
    to share my faith 0 1 2 3 4 5

Evangelism Total   _____

Spiritual Health Plan

After completing the Spiritual Health Assessment, you can create a plan for growth in each of God's purposes. Start with Fellowship and Discipleship as those are the two areas we've discussed so far. Pick one next step for each of the areas. Then each week you can pick one more next step with your spiritual partner for that week's area.

Purpose	Next Step
Fellowship: Deepening my relationships with others.	
Discipleship: Growing to be like Christ.	
Ministry: Serving others with my God-given shape.	
Worship: Connecting with God	
Evangelism: Sharing the story of what God's done in my life.